ANIMALS OF THE ARCTIC

Snowy Owls

by Betsy Rathburn

BELLWETHER MEDIA • MINNEAPOLIS, MN

BLASTOFF!
2
READERS

Blastoff! Readers are carefully developed by literacy experts to build reading stamina and move students toward fluency by combining standards-based content with developmentally appropriate text.

Level 1 provides the most support through repetition of high-frequency words, light text, predictable sentence patterns, and strong visual support.

Level 2 offers early readers a bit more challenge through varied sentences, increased text load, and text-supportive special features.

Level 3 advances early-fluent readers toward fluency through increased text load, less reliance on photos, advancing concepts, longer sentences, and more complex special features.

★ **Blastoff! Universe**

Reading Level

Grade K → Grades 1-3 → Grade 4

This edition first published in 2021 by Bellwether Media, Inc.

No part of this publication may be reproduced in whole or in part without written permission of the publisher. For information regarding permission, write to Bellwether Media, Inc., Attention: Permissions Department, 6012 Blue Circle Drive, Minnetonka, MN 55343.

Library of Congress Cataloging-in-Publication Data

Names: Rathburn, Betsy, author.
Title: Snowy owls / by Betsy Rathburn.
Description: Minneapolis, MN : Bellwether Media, Inc., 2021. | Series: Blast off! readers: animals of the Arctic | Includes bibliographical references and index. | Audience: Ages 5-8 | Audience: Grades K-1 |
   Summary: "Relevant images match informative text in this introduction to snowy owls. Intended for students in kindergarten through third grade"-- Provided by publisher.
   Identifiers: LCCN 2019053742 (print) | LCCN 2019053743 (ebook) | ISBN 9781644872147 (library binding) | ISBN 9781618919724 (ebook)
Subjects: LCSH: Snowy owl--Juvenile literature. | Zoology--Arctic regions--Juvenile literature.
Classification: LCC QL696.S83 R38 2021 (print) | LCC QL696.S83 (ebook) | DDC 598.9/709113--dc23
LC record available at https://lccn.loc.gov/2019053742
LC ebook record available at https://lccn.loc.gov/2019053743

Editor: Kieran Downs   Designer: Brittany McIntosh

Printed in the United States of America, North Mankato, MN

Table of
Contents

Life in the Arctic

Snowy owls are cold weather survivors. They are known for their white feathers.

These birds **glide** over open **tundra**. They are found in the Arctic.

Snowy Owl Range

range =

The Arctic is snowy and cold. Snowy owls have **adapted** to this **biome**.

White feathers help them blend in.
Other animals cannot see them
against snow!

Snowy owls have feathered feet.
This keeps their toes warm.

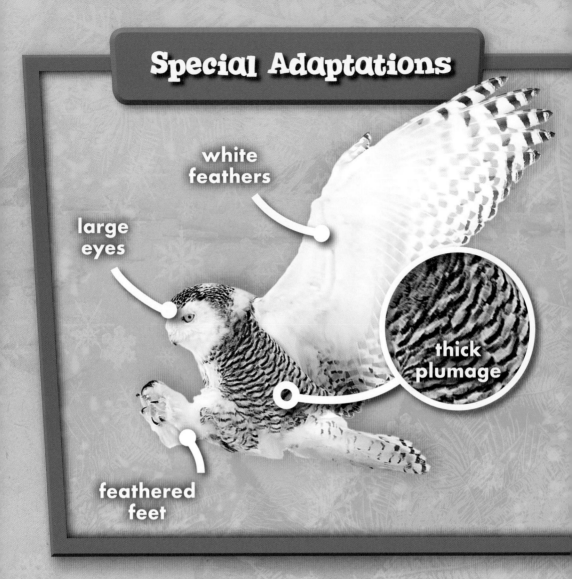

Special Adaptations

white feathers

large eyes

thick plumage

feathered feet

Thick **plumage** keeps their bodies warm. These owls are made for the cold!

Snowy owls are **diurnal**.
But Arctic winters are dark
all day.

These owls see well in the dark. Their big eyes let in a lot of light!

11

Snowy owls travel often.
They fly through their
territories in search
of food.

Fringed wing feathers
help them fly without
a sound.

Snowy owls are **solitary**. But they sometimes **communicate** with other owls.

They hoot to find **mates** and
mark territory.

Swooping for Food

Snowy owls are **carnivores**. They wait on branches for food to come near.

They can **swivel** their heads in almost a complete circle. This gives them a full view!

Snowy Owl Stats

Least Concern	Near Threatened	Vulnerable	Endangered	Critically Endangered	Extinct in the Wild	Extinct

conservation status: vulnerable

life span: up to 10 years

17

talons

When food comes close,
snowy owls dive!

They pick up **prey** in their sharp **talons**. Lemmings are a favorite meal.

Snowy Owl Diet

rock ptarmigans

Arctic hares

northern collared lemmings

Hooked beaks keep prey from escaping. Snowy owls swallow their food whole.

These birds were made for the Arctic biome!

Glossary

adapted—changed over a long period of time

biome—a large area with certain plants, animals, and weather

carnivores—animals that only eat meat

communicate—to share information and feelings

diurnal—active in the daytime

fringed—having a border of fine feathers

glide—to move smoothly

mates—partners

plumage—the feathers of a bird

prey—animals that are hunted by other animals for food

solitary—living alone

swivel—to turn smoothly; snowy owls can swivel their heads in almost a complete circle.

talons—the claws of a snowy owl

territories—land areas where animals live

tundra—rocky land in the Arctic that has a frozen layer

To Learn More

AT THE LIBRARY

Cocca, Lisa Colozza. *Tundra Animals*. Vero Beach, Fla.: Rourke Educational Media, 2019.

Hansen, Grace. *Snowy Owl*. Minneapolis, Minn.: Abdo Kids, 2020.

Suen, Anastasia. *Snowy Owls*. Mankato, Minn.: Amicus, 2020.

ON THE WEB

FACTSURFER

Factsurfer.com gives you a safe, fun way to find more information.

1. Go to www.factsurfer.com.

2. Enter "snowy owls" into the search box and click 🔍.

3. Select your book cover to see a list of related content.

23

Index

The images in this book are reproduced through the courtesy of: FotoRequest, front cover; Jim Cumming, pp. 4, 9, 12, 18; RT Images, p. 6; AlesVeluscek, p. 7; David G Hemmings/ Getty Images, p. 8; Chris Hill, p. 10; Erick Margarita Images, p. 11; rpbirdman, p. 13; Firma V, pp. 14, 23; LesPalenik, p. 15; Guoqiang Xue, p. 16; Francis Bossé, p. 17; feathercollector, p. 19 (rock ptarmigan); Jukka Jantunen, p. 19 (Arctic hare); All Canada Photos/ Alamy, p. 19 (northern collared lemming); WILDLIFE GmbH/ Alamy, p. 20; UrbanRadim, p. 21.